Groovy

Graphing

Lisa Arias

Rourke
Educational Media

rourkeeducationalmedia.com

Scan for Related Titles
and Teacher Resources

Before Reading:

Building Academic Vocabulary and Background Knowledge

Before reading a book, it is important to tap into what your child or students already know about the topic. This will help them develop their vocabulary, increase their reading comprehension, and make connections across the curriculum.

1. *Look at the cover of the book. What will this book be about?*
2. *What do you already know about the topic?*
3. *Let's study the Table of Contents. What will you learn about in the book's chapters?*
4. *What would you like to learn about this topic? Do you think you might learn about it from this book? Why or why not?*
5. *Use a reading journal to write about your knowledge of this topic. Record what you already know about the topic and what you hope to learn about the topic.*
6. *Read the book.*
7. *In your reading journal, record what you learned about the topic and your response to the book.*
8. *After reading the book complete the activities below.*

Content Area Vocabulary
Read the list. What do these words mean?

Cartesian coordinate system
coordinate
coordinate plane
negative numbers
ordered pairs
plane
plot
point of origin
quadrants
scale
x- axis
x-coordinate
y- axis
y-coordinate

After Reading:

Comprehension and Extension Activity

After reading the book, work on the following questions with your child or students in order to check their level of reading comprehension and content mastery.

1. *In an ordered pair, what is the first number called? The second number? (Summarize)*
2. *In what ways does skip counting make graphing easier? (Summarize)*
3. *Why are quadrant names written with Roman Numerals instead of numbers? (Asking questions)*
4. *Explain how you would plot an ordered pair on a graph? (Determining importance)*
5. *Where do the x- axis and y- axis intersect? (Summarize)*

Extension Activity

Using graph paper draw any polygon. Place a dot at each vertex. Now write an ordered pair for each vertex on a separate sheet of paper. Give your coordinates to a partner to see if they can create the same polygon using only your coordinates.

Table of Contents

Cartesian Coordinate System

The **Cartesian coordinate system** is what graphing is all about.

Before it was invented, there was no way to explain the exact location of things without the help of a scout.

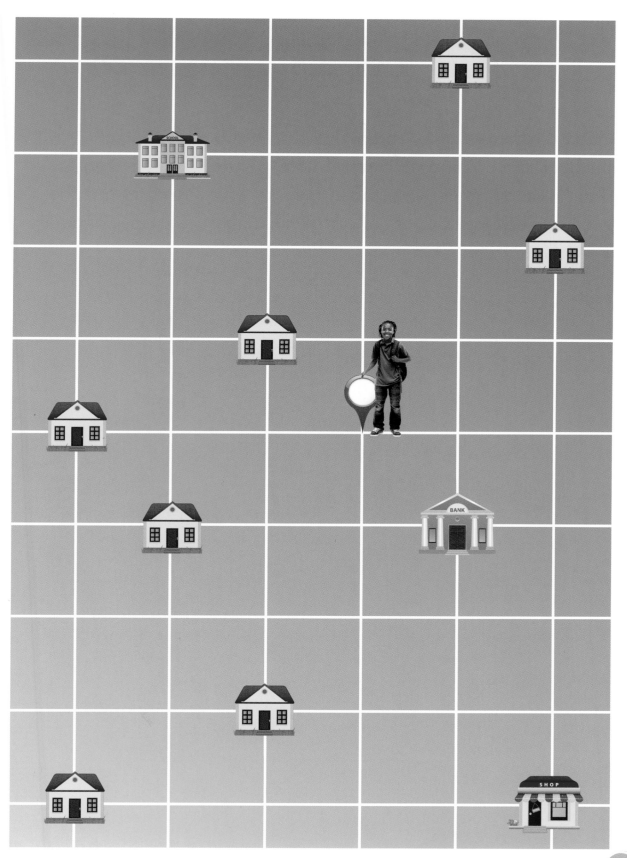

Coordinate Planes

The **coordinate** system pinpoints places and things using numbers and points on a **coordinate plane**. The coordinate plane is made up of two number lines called the **x-axis** and the **y-axis**. They intersect at the **point of origin**. This special point is where everything begins.

Check It Out!

The y-axis stands vertical

The x-axis runs horizontal

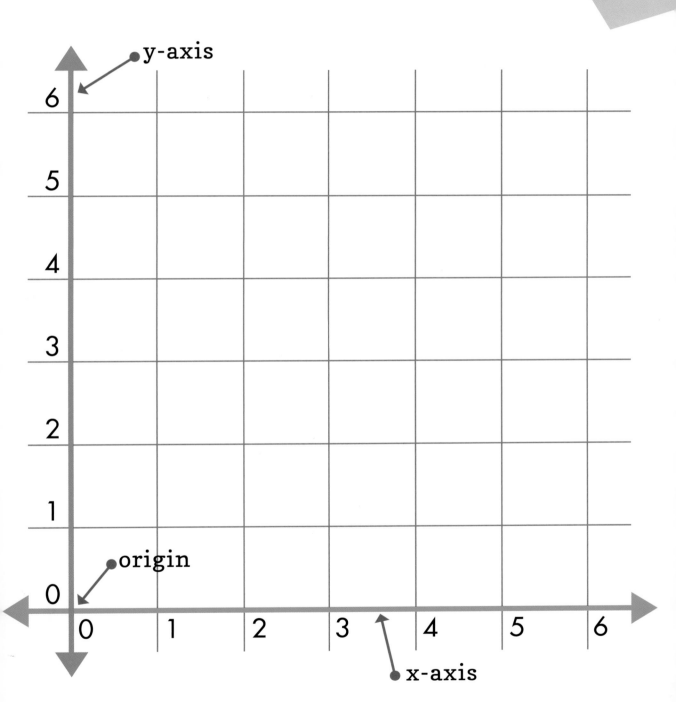

Ordered Pairs

Ordered pairs are just the right friends for plotting points. Each ordered pair has two numbers. The **x-coordinate** is the first number of the pair, followed by the **y-coordinate**, who I hear is very dear.

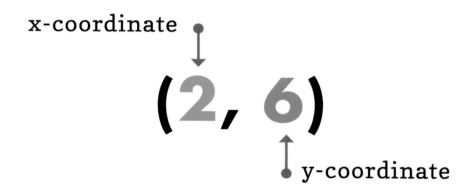

Please group coordinates in parenthesis and use a comma to avoid any drama!

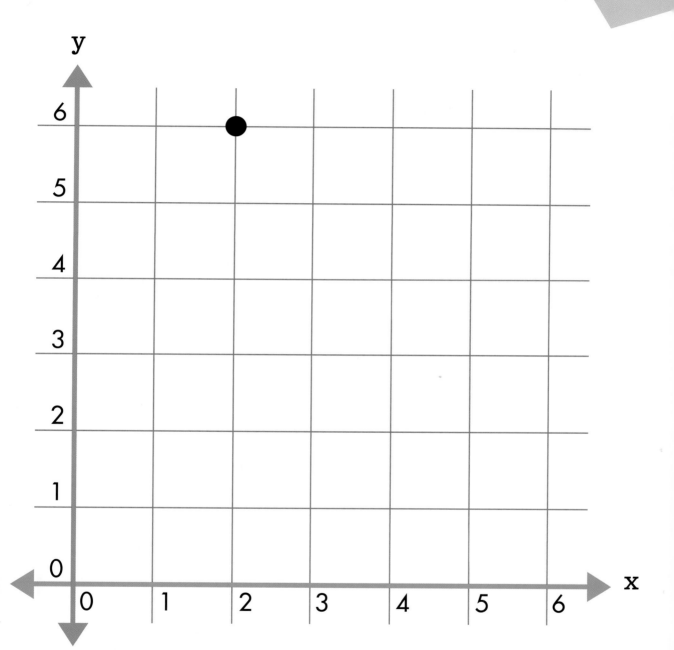

Plotting Coordinates

Each coordinate is graphed on its matching axis.

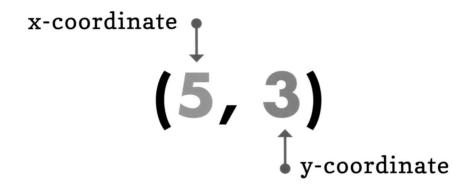

x-coordinate

(5, 3)

y-coordinate

To graph the x-coordinate:
Start from the point of origin. Hop across the x-axis to the spot that fits the x-coordinate.

To graph the y-coordinate:
Start again from the point of origin. Rise or fall along the tall y-axis to the spot that fits the y-coordinate.

*To **plot** the spot:*
Next, slide your fingers from each spot to find the intersecting point.

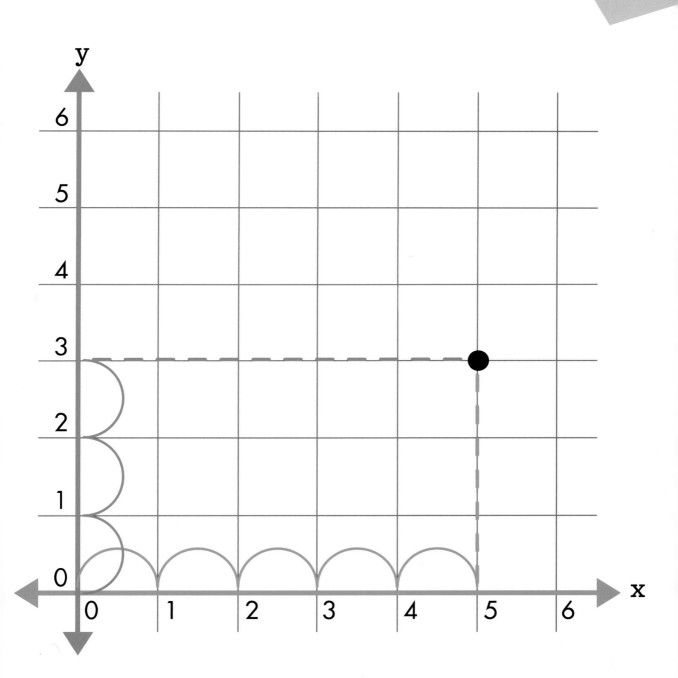

Plotting Practice

Name each ordered pair.

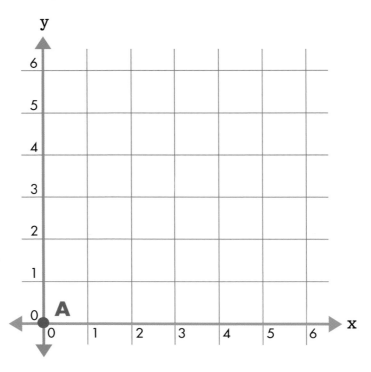

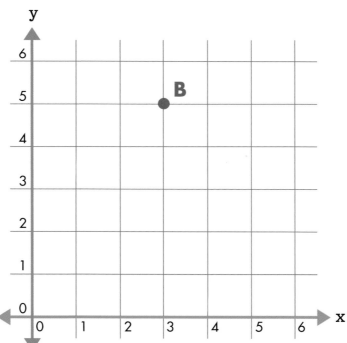

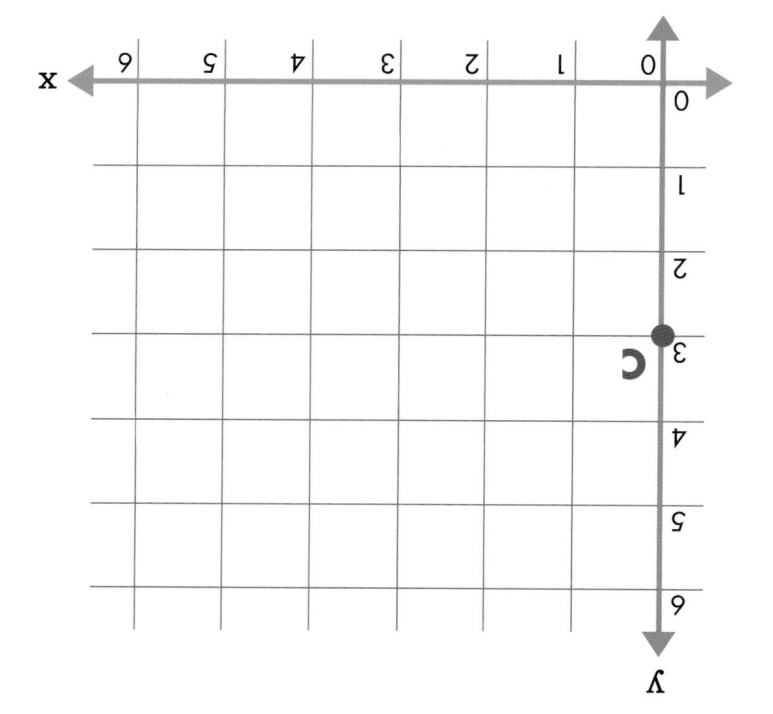

13

Answers:

A **(0,0)** point of origin   C **(0,3)**

B **(3,5)**   D **(4,1)**

Creating a Scale

It takes some practice
to create a number line for each axis.
Instead of numbering one by one,
skip count by the best amount and you're done.
Skip counting creates a **scale**,
making graphs easy to read without fail.

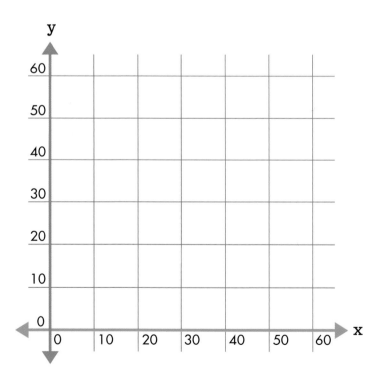

Skip count by tens.

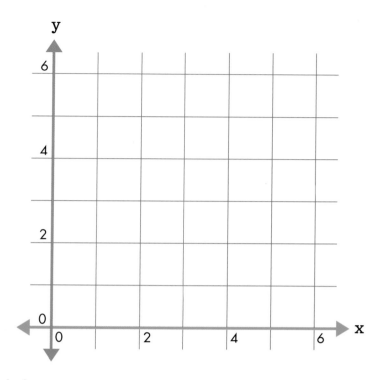

Skip count both by twos.

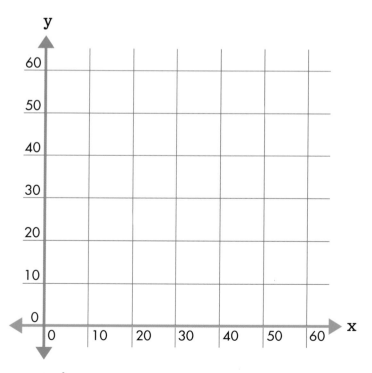

Skip count the y-axis by tens.

Graph Between Points

When needed, estimate the spot for your dot between the two closest points.

Graph:

(7.5, 5)

Since 7.5 is not a point on the x-axis, place it halfway between points 7 and 8.

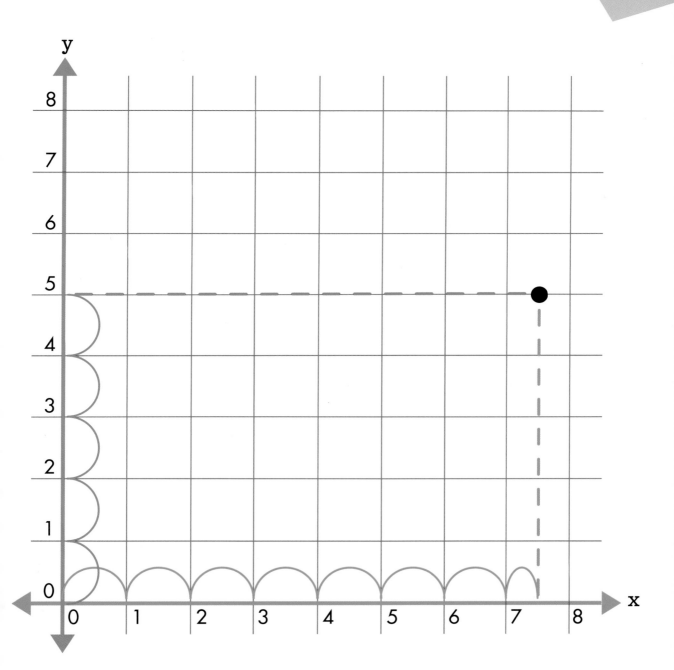

The Four Quadrants

The coordinate plane is divided into four sections called **quadrants**. The four quadrants are there to help plot **negative numbers** from your ordered pair.

Each quadrant is labeled in Roman Numerals. Their order follows the shape of the letter C, quite conveniently.

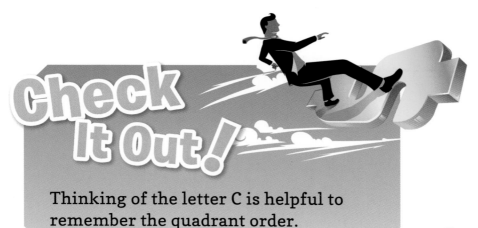

Thinking of the letter C is helpful to remember the quadrant order.

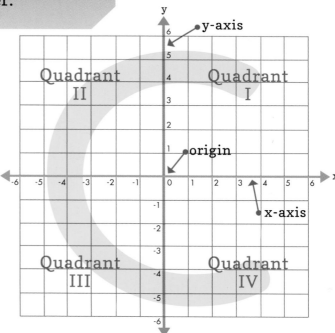

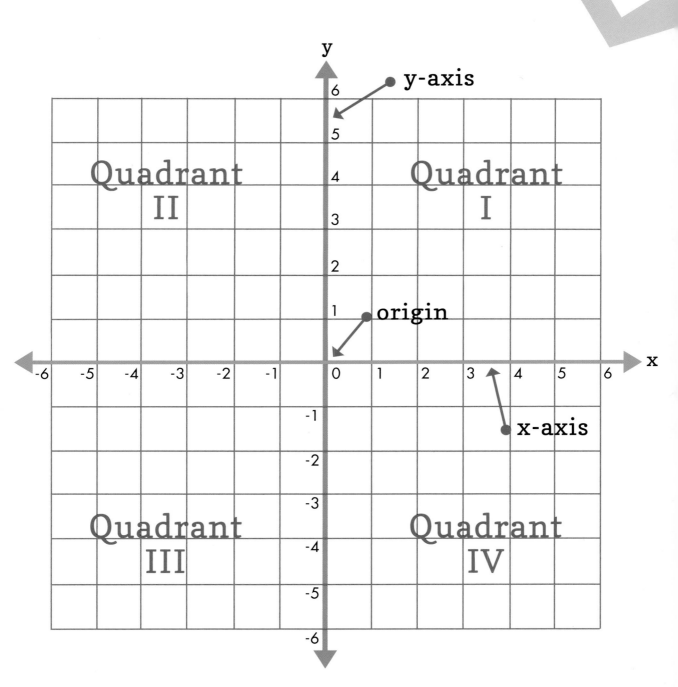

Four Quadrant Ordered Pairs

To plot an ordered pair, get a head start on the location by checking the x and y combination.

Quadrant	Positive or Negative x and y coordinates	Example
Quadrant I	x and y are both positive (+, +)	(6, 1)
Quadrant II	x is negative and y is positive (-, +)	(-3, 4)
Quadrant III	x and y are both negative (-, -)	(-5, -2)
Quadrant IV	x is positive and y is negative (+, -)	(4, -5)
No Quadrant	Any ordered pair containing a zero will lie directly on an axis.	(0, 0) (0, 3) (-1, 0)

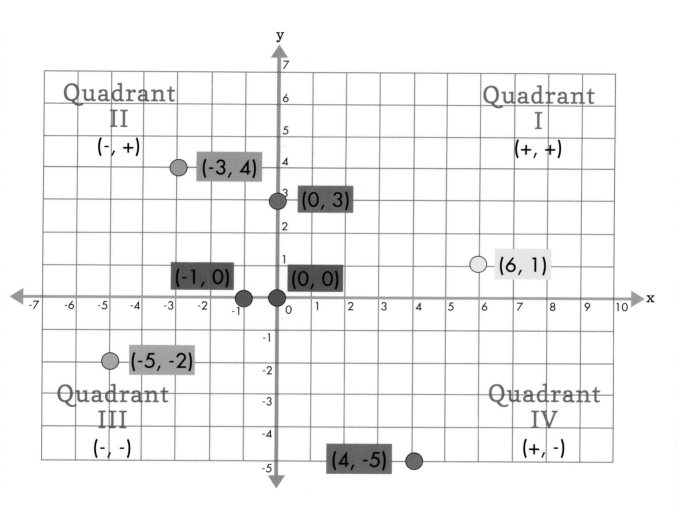

Name the Quadrant

Name the quadrant or axis for each ordered pair.

(0,18)

(21, -15)

(-9, 99)

(27, 0)

(-14, -3)

(9,16)

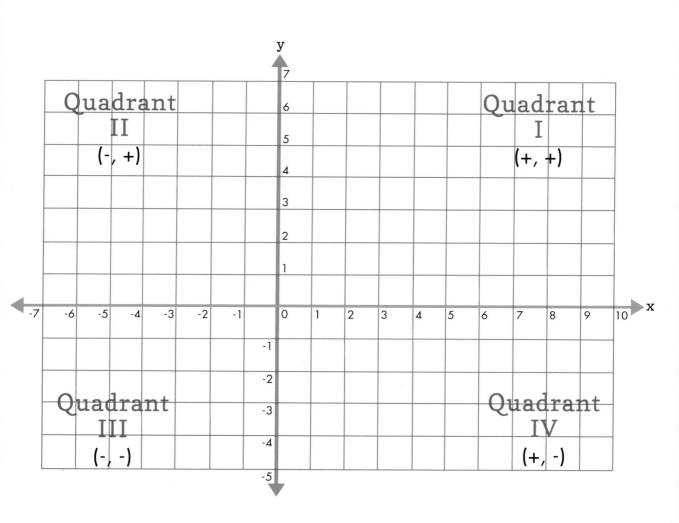

Answers:

Quadrant I
Quadrant III
x-axis

Quadrant II
Quadrant IV
y-axis

Four Quadrant Graphing

Name each ordered pair.

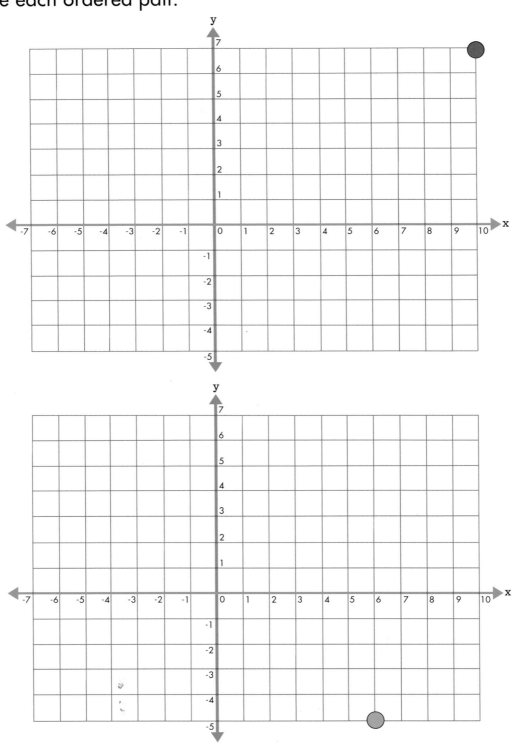

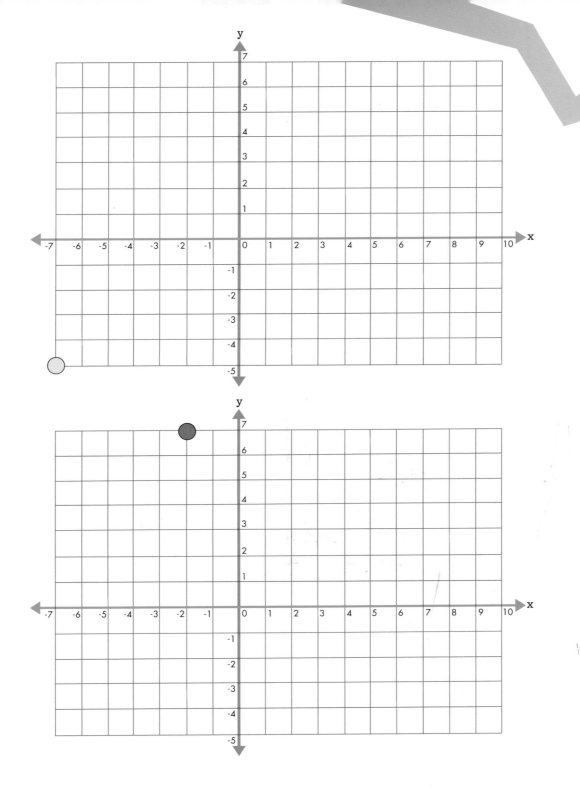

Coordinate Graphs and Maps

When giving directions to places on a coordinate plane, include the direction of travel and count the hops you make from spot to spot. Let's take a moment to explain the directions and distance when traveling from the park to the school.

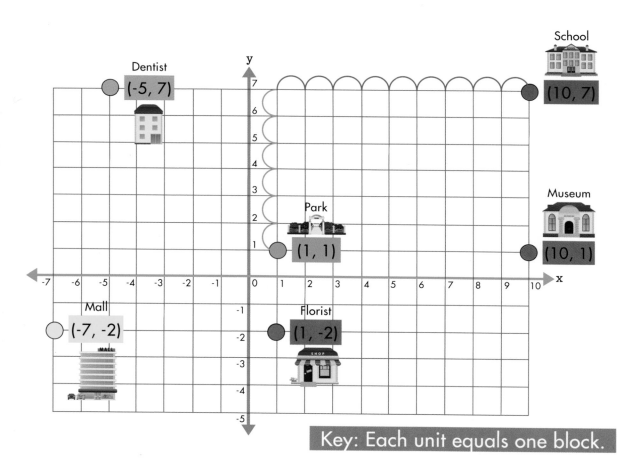

Key: Each unit equals one block.

The school is north of the park, so begin by traveling north for 6 blocks. Next travel east for 9 blocks until you are at the school. The distance traveled was a total of 15 blocks.

Explain the directions and distance from the dentist to the park.

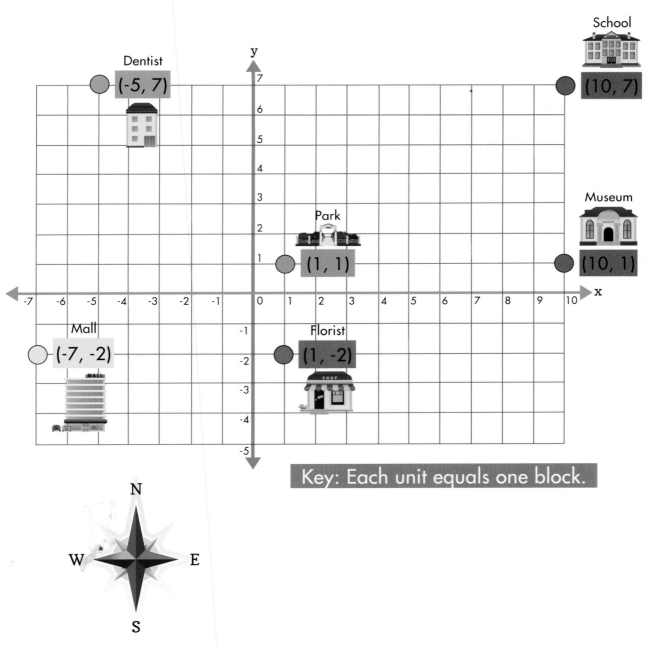

Key: Each unit equals one block.

Dentist (-5, 7)
School (10, 7)
Museum (10, 1)
Park (1, 1)
Mall (-7, -2)
Florist (1, -2)

N
W   E
S

Answer: Travel south for 6 blocks and then east for 6 blocks for a total of 12 blocks.

Find the Distance

You can compare the coordinates of ordered pairs to find the distance between two places on a map.

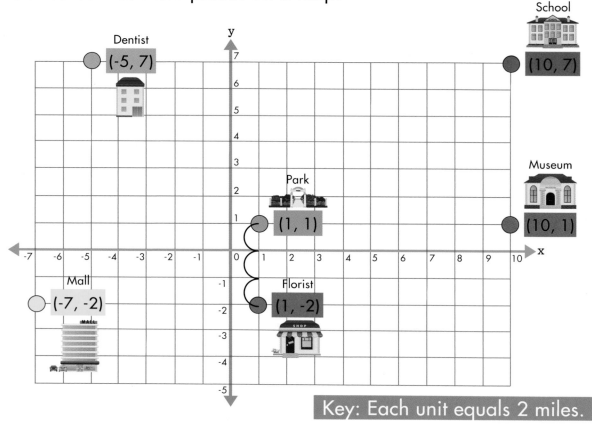

Key: Each unit equals 2 miles.

Find the distance between the florist and the park. The florist and the park share the same x-coordinate. To find the distance between each place, count the three hops between the two spots along the y-axis.

Multiply each hop by two miles.

> 3 spots
> × 2 miles for each spot
> _____
> 6 miles is the distance between the park and the florist.

Find the distance between the school and the museum.
Find the distance between the dentist and the school.
Find the distance between the park and the museum.

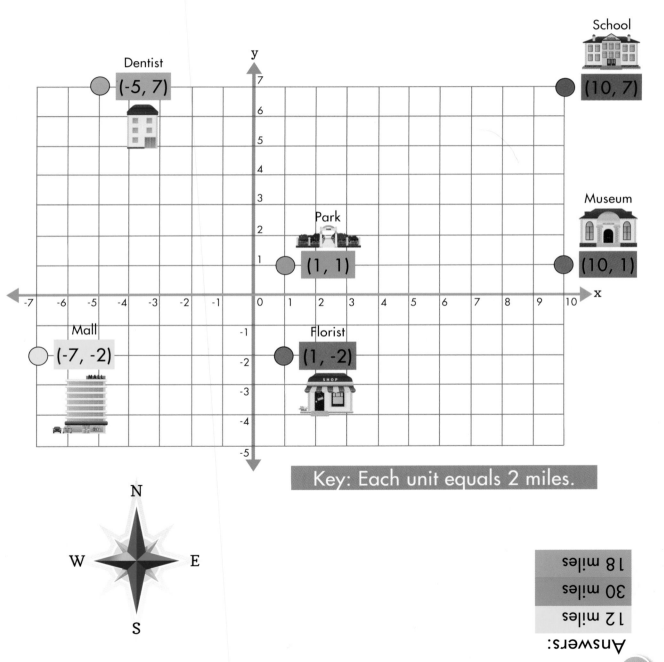

Key: Each unit equals 2 miles.

Glossary

Cartesian coordinate system (kahr-TEE-zhuhn koh-OR-duh-nate SISS-tuhm): a plane made up of an x-axis and y-axis that shows the exact position of places and things

coordinate (koh-OR-duh-nate): a number used to show the point on a number line or graph

coordinate plane (koh-OR-duh-nate PLANE): an endless flat surface made up of an x-axis and y-axis that shows the exact positions of places and things

negative numbers (NEG-uh-tiv NUHM-burz): numbers less than zero

ordered pairs (OR-durd PAIRZ): a pair of numbers used to find a point on a coordinate

plane (PLANE): an endless flat surface

plot (PLOT): to mark

point of origin (POINT uv OR-uh-jin): the point where the x-axis and y-axis intersect on a coordinate graph

quadrants (KWAHD-ruhnts): the four areas created when the x-axis and y-axis intersect on a coordinate graph

scale (SKALE): the size of the something that is being measured

x-axis (EKS AK-siss): the line that runs horizontally in a coordinate plane

x-coordinate (EKS koh-OR-duh-nate): the first number in an ordered pair

y-axis (WYE AK-siss): the line that runs vertically in a coordinate plane

y-coordinate (WYE koh-OR-duh-nate): the second number in an ordered pair

Index

Websites to Visit

www.hotmath.com/hotmath_help/games/ctf/ctf_hotmath.swf

www.mathplayground.com/locate_aliens.html

www.mrnussbaum.com/stockshelves1

About the Author

Lisa Arias is a math teacher who lives in Tampa, Florida with her husband and two children. Her out-of-the-box thinking and love for math guided her toward becoming an author. She enjoys playing board games and spending time with family and friends.

Meet The Author!
www.meetREMauthors.com

www.rourkeeducationalmedia.com

PHOTO CREDITS: Cover: © Draco77, Andynwt; Page 4: © Yuri_Arcurs; Page 5: © Saransk; Page 6: © Draco77; Page 20: © Saransk; Page 27: © ildogesto

Edited by: Jill Sherman

Cover and Interior design by: Tara Raymo

Library of Congress PCN Data

Groovy Graphing: Quadrant One and Beyond / Lisa Arias
(Got Math!)
ISBN 978-1-62717-720-7 (hard cover)
ISBN 978-1-62717-842-6 (soft cover)
ISBN 978-1-62717-955-3 (e-Book)
Library of Congress Control Number: 2014935600

Printed in the United States of America, North Mankato, Minnesota

Also Available as:

ROURKE'S e-Books

1716